Oh, t...  a Web!

by Brenda Chan
illustrated by Brandon Reese

⊠Harcourt
SCHOOL PUBLISHERS

Printed in China

ISBN 10: 0-15-350689-X
ISBN 13: 978-0-15-350689-5

Ordering Options
ISBN 10: 0-15-350600-8 (Grade 3 On-Level Collection)
ISBN 13: 978-0-15-350600-0 (Grade 3 On-Level Collection)
ISBN 10: 0-15-357910-2 (package of 5)
ISBN 13: 978-0-15-357910-3 (package of 5)

11 12 13 14 15 0940 12 11 10

Sally was a very young spider. She lived on
a farm with her mother and many farm animals.
Sally had a problem, though. She could not spin
a web. Sally's mother spun excellent webs. One
day Sally's mother set out to teach Sally everything
she knew.

"The first thing to remember, Sally," began her
mother, "is that you have to find a high place to
jump from. Climb up to the rafters, please. That's
a good spot right there."

Sally's mother continued with her instructions.
"Next, make sure that there is a wind blowing.
It will help to carry you from place to place. At
the count of 'three,' jump with all your might. As
you jump, let out some strands. As you pass a
crossbeam, the strands should stick to it."

Summoning all her nerve, Sally closed her
eyes. Her mother began to count, "One . . . two . . .
three!" Sally jumped with all her might.

To her disappointment, Sally's spinnerets had
not worked. She had not stuck to a crossbeam.
She had not spun a web. Instead, she had fallen
straight down and landed in a large pile of hay.

"Oh, what a nuisance it is to build a web! When
will I ever learn?" Sally wondered crossly. She had
wanted to oblige her mother by learning quickly.
Instead, she felt as if she would never learn. Sally
felt very shaken up and rather glum.

"Mom, the room is spinning," Sally moaned. "My head is spinning, too. Why can't I spin a web?"

"It will happen sooner or later," said her mother calmly. "Take a deep breath and don't worry about it, Sally, dear."

This went on for more than a week. Sally's mother repeated the instructions over and over. She showed Sally every web-building trick she knew. By now, there were webs all over the barn. However, not a single one of them belonged to Sally.

One afternoon Sally overheard Percival, the
barnyard pig, and Mory, the mouse, talking.

Mory was boasting, as usual. "If *I* could teach
Sally, she would be building beautiful webs
by now."

Percival was annoyed. "You are one of the
laziest animals I know. In fact, you don't even find
your own food. All you do is eat the scraps that I
leave for you."

"You are the sedentary one," replied the mouse.
"I actually clean up after you by eating your scraps!
You should thank me for doing you a favor. No,
Percival, it is clear to me that Sally simply does
not have the touch."

Sally was shocked and ashamed at what she
heard. Anyway, she knew they had not meant for
her to overhear. She crept away silently to think.
Slowly, leg over leg over leg over leg, she picked
her way across the yard and over to the barn.

"How nice it would be to have a web full of dinner waiting for me," she thought hungrily. "First I would have to spin a web. As Mory says, I simply do not have the touch."

Then Sally had a new thought. She pulled herself together. She said out loud, "What would a barnyard mouse know about making a spider web anyway?"

This time she didn't even have to think about it. Two silvery, thin threads came out from her spinnerets.

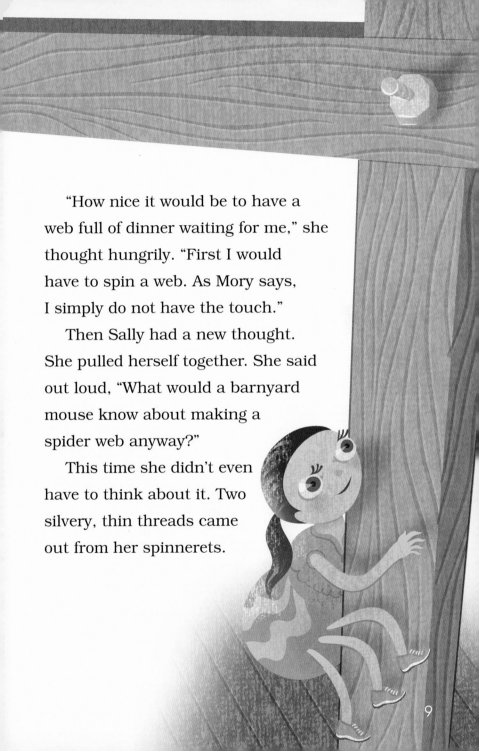

Sally sailed gracefully through the air. She floated until she reached a crossbeam. The threads stuck tight. Success! The jumping part was over. Sally was hanging in midair. She could even sway gracefully from side to side.

In her mind, Sally reviewed all the lessons her mother had taught her. She closed her eyes and gathered her eight legs beneath her.

One . . . two . . . three! Sally leaped off the rafters and flew into the air.

"Now, let me think. What did mother say to do next?" Sally was very excited. "Oh, yes, attach, climb, attach, slide."

Sally repeated this pattern over and over again. The web—and it was now a web for sure—grew larger, wider, and rounder.

After a few hours, the web was completely done. Sally scurried to a far corner of the web. She watched and waited because she was eager to see what would happen next.

A short time later, Percival strolled into the
barn and glanced up at the rafters. He immediately
noticed the web's sparkling strands. "Who made
that amazing web?" he wondered admiringly.

Next, Mory scurried in. He was on the lookout
for something to munch on, as usual. He spotted
Percival. "Scraps," he thought with glee as he
scampered over to his friend.

Percival paid him no attention. Instead, he continued to stare at the new web in the rafters. Mory followed his gaze, up, up, up, until he, too, saw the web.

"What a lovely work of art!" thought Mory, though he would never say so out loud. "Sally's mother is getting better every day."

Finally, Sally's mother came into the barn. She looked at the web in the rafters and let out a little gasp.

"Sally! Is that your web?" her mother exclaimed.

Sally blushed as only a spider can. "Do you like it, Mom?"

"Indeed I do," her mom said. "I was going to call you for supper, but I think you will do just fine at catching your own."

Sally ended her day with a full stomach, many compliments, and a beautiful web. She had tried and failed and tried again, and her determination had paid off at last.

Think Critically

1. How do Sally's feelings about making webs change during the story?

2. What is the theme of this story?

3. Where does this story take place?

4. Which parts of this story could not happen in real life? Which parts could happen in real life?

5. What would you say to Mory, the mouse, after he questions Sally's ability to build a web?

 Science

Find Out About Spiders Look up information about different kinds of spiders. Then make a chart that tells about where they live, what they eat, and any other information that interests you.

 School-Home Connection Make a list of things you would like to learn or to teach somebody else. Choose one item on the list. Think of the next step you could take to learn or to teach this skill. Share your idea with a family member.

Word Count: 926